YAMAHA CHRISTMAS ENSEMBLES

A collection of 19 favorite carols that correlates page-by-page with the Yamaha Band Student, Books **& 2**

D1469619

John O'Reilly
John Kinyon

The YAMAHA CHRISTMAS ENSEMBLES are designed to parallel Books One and Two of the YAMAHA BAND STUDENT. Each ensemble page is correlated to the method, thus enabling the teacher to easily find and reinforce those materials previously taught.

This ensemble folio will serve not only to motivate beginning band students in the classroom, but also to encourage home and neighborhood combos as well.

YAMAHA CHRISTMAS ENSEMBLES can be performed by a wide variety of instrumental combinations.

Line A is always the melody part, to be used for solos.

Line B is always the preferred harmony part, to be used for duets.

Line C is always the bass part, to be used for trios and/or full band ensembles.

A simple but effective piano accompaniment is provided in the score.

Contents

Instrumentation

Flute/Oboe
B♭ Clarinet/Bass Clarinet
E♭ Alto/Baritone Saxophone
B♭ Tenor Sax
B♭ Trumpet/Baritone T.C.
Horn In F
Trombone/Baritone B.C./Bassoon
Tuba
Percussion
Conductor's Score/Piano Accompaniment

YAMAHA®
is a registered trademark of
Yamaha Corporation of America

Cover photograph: Jordan Miller
Art direction: Ruth McKinney/Ted Engelbart
Interior production supervision: Tom Gerou

Hark! The Herald Angels Sing

O Come, O Come Emmanuel

We Three Kings

Andante

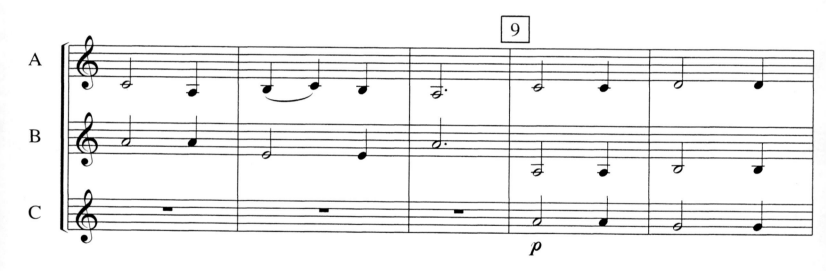

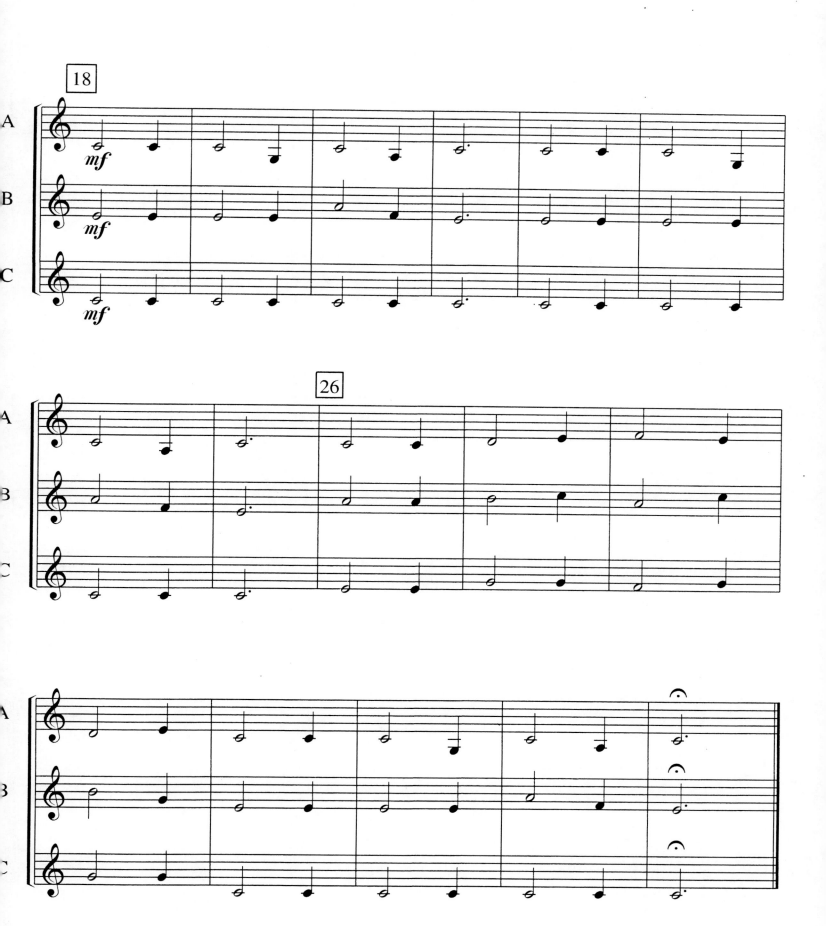

Away in a Manger

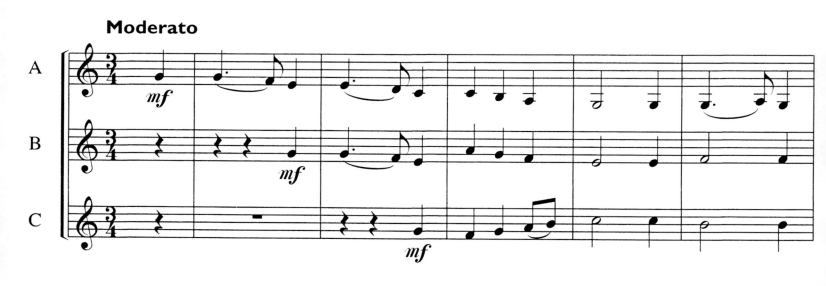

Good King Wenceslas

Allegro

Angels We Have Heard on High

Moderato

God Rest Ye Merry, Gentlemen

In the Bleak Mid-Winter

Jolly Old St. Nicholas

It Came upon a Midnight Clear

Jingle Bells

While Shepherds Watched Their Flocks

Andante

We Wish You a Merry Christmas

Allegretto

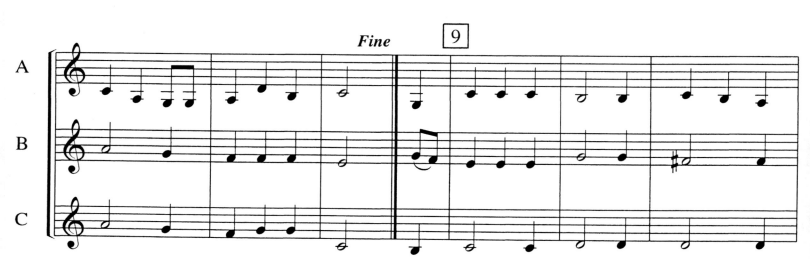

Deck the Halls

O Come, Little Children

Up on the Housetop

Go Tell It on the Mountain

Lo, How a Rose

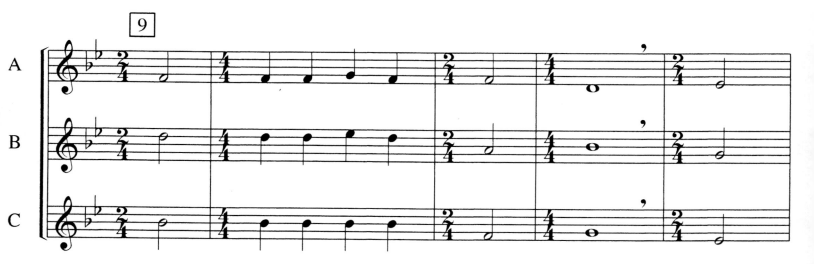

Silent Night